D1269104

JIM BURNS

How God Makes Babies

BETHANY HOUSE PUBLISHERS
Minneapolis, Minnesota

DEDICATED TO
Dean Bruns
Your partnership in ministry means so much.

SPECIAL THANKS TO OUR ADVISORY PANEL:

Jennifer Degler, PhD

Nicole Frye, MA, LPC

Sandi Hofer, MA

Karl Williams, MD

How God Makes Babies
Copyright © 2009
Jim Burns

Cover design by Lookout Design, Inc.

Interior design by Melinda Schumacher.

Scripture quotations identified ICB are taken from the International Children's Bible®. Copyright © 1986, 1988, 1999 by Thomas Nelson, Inc. Used by permission. All rights reserved.

Scripture quotations identified GW is taken from God's Word®. © 1995 by God's Word to the Nations. Used by permission of Baker Publishing Group. All rights reserved.

Published by Bethany House Publishers
11400 Hampshire Avenue South
Bloomington, MN 55438

Bethany House Publishers is a division of
Baker Publishing Group, Grand Rapids, Michigan.

Printed in China.

ISBN 978-0-7642-0210-0

Library of Congress Cataloging-in-Publication Data is available for this title.

A Special Note to Parents

Studies show that when children receive values-centered sex education at home, they are less likely to become sexually promiscuous and more likely to have a healthy view of their bodies and relationships. With the media introducing sexual topics to children at such a young age, there is no better countermeasure than parents introducing the concepts in this book to their children.

This book is part of a series of developmentally appropriate books called PURE FOUNDATIONS. *How God Makes Babies* is specifically geared for children ages 6 to 9. As you know, kids this age are extremely curious. This book will answer some of their questions and give you the opportunity to answer more. Experts tell us this is a key age to talk about the basics and give God-honoring instruction. One of the greatest benefits of teaching them at this age is establishing a healthy trust, demonstrating that you are willing to bring up the issues and that they can come to you for more dialogue. If the information doesn't come from you, your children will learn it from the Internet or other unfiltered sources.

Obviously, a book of this length will not cover every subject. It is meant to help you and your child develop a loving, trusting relationship where dialogue is the best teacher. And you'll discover spontaneous teaching moments from TV or other avenues to continue reinforcing a healthy view of sexuality.

Thanks for laying a foundation of trust and honesty with your child. You are giving your child a gift that will serve him for a lifetime.

Jim Burns, PhD

Do you know a family that is expecting a baby?

Maybe it's your own family and you'll soon have a new brother or sister.

When a family is expecting a new baby, it's an exciting time. Everyone is busy making plans! Mom might have ideas for decorating the new baby's room. Maybe Dad has started a list of baby names. Grandmas and grandpas, uncles and aunts—everyone else in the family probably has suggestions too!

God's plan for families began when He created Adam and Eve. God created Eve so that Adam wouldn't be alone and so that they could start a family together.

Ever since Adam and Eve, when a man and a woman love each other and want to be together always, they get married.

Have you ever been to a wedding? At a wedding, a man and a woman stand up together in front of their family and friends. They make a promise to God and to each other to always love and honor each other. Then they are husband and wife!

A husband and wife show their love for each other in many ways.

They live together. They share their deepest thoughts with each other. They pray together. They encourage each other. They make decisions together.

One of God's great ideas for a husband and wife was to make a way for them to join their bodies together. A husband and wife kiss and cuddle and hold each other in ways they would not do with any other person. They get as close as two people can get. It's called *making love* or *having sex*. It's something God created just for a husband and wife to enjoy when they are alone together.

Every little girl is born with a vagina and a womb.

A girl's vagina is inside of her body between her legs. It is connected to her womb or *uterus*. The womb is the safe place inside a mother where a baby grows before it is born. A girl also has two *ovaries* that connect to her uterus by two *Fallopian tubes*. Inside the two ovaries are thousands of tiny eggs.

Because of these special parts, girls can grow up to become mothers.

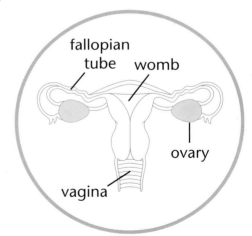

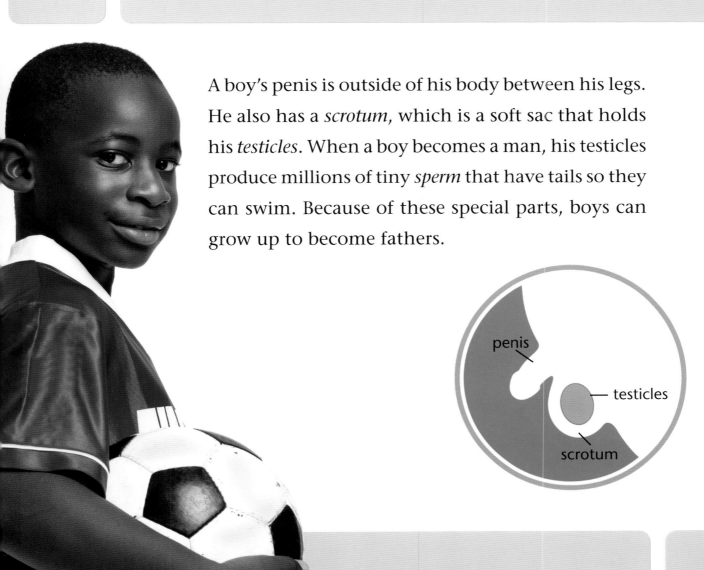

Every little boy is born with a penis.

A boy's penis is outside of his body between his legs. He also has a *scrotum*, which is a soft sac that holds his *testicles*. When a boy becomes a man, his testicles produce millions of tiny *sperm* that have tails so they can swim. Because of these special parts, boys can grow up to become fathers.

penis

testicles

scrotum

These special parts that girls have and the special parts that boys have are also called *private* parts. They are the parts covered by your underwear or swimsuit. When something is private, it is not meant to be shared with other people. For your private parts, that means other people are not allowed to touch or look at them. The only exceptions are these:

- As part of your checkup, your doctor or nurse might need to look at or touch your private parts to make sure you are healthy.
- When you are young, your mom or dad may need to help you in the bath to keep your private parts clean.

16

If anyone else ever tries to touch your private parts or asks you to touch their private parts, tell that person to stop. No matter who it is, even if it's a friend or someone in your family, they are not allowed to touch you in any way that makes you uncomfortable. If this happens, tell a grown-up you trust right away.

Sharing your private parts is something to save for your husband or wife when you are grown and married. That is God's wonderful plan.

> *[A husband and wife] will become one body.*
>
> — Genesis 2:24b (ICB)

Now, a woman cannot become a mother all by herself. And a man cannot become a father all by himself. The egg from a woman's body must come together with the sperm from a man's body in order to make a baby. This happens when a man and a woman make love. It's all part of God's creation and the miracle of how children are born.

When a husband and wife make love, they fit together in a wonderful way. The husband puts his penis into the wife's vagina. It might sound icky or uncomfortable to you, and that's okay. Making love is a beautiful thing meant only for grown-ups who are married to each other.

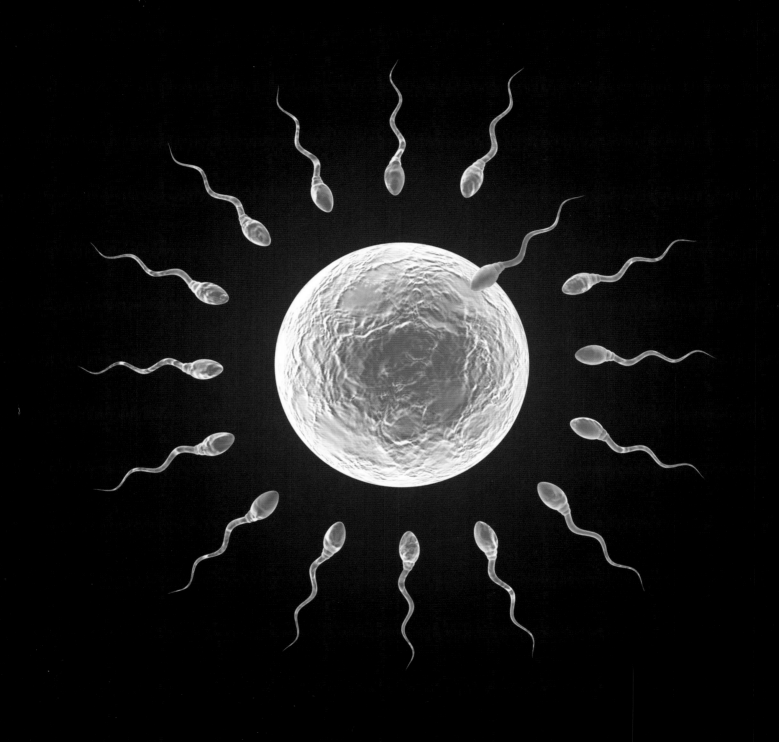

When a couple makes love, millions of sperm come out of the man's penis. The sperm have tails to help them swim through the woman's vagina and uterus and into her Fallopian tubes. The sperm are looking for an egg that comes from the woman's ovaries.

It's like a race to see which sperm gets to the egg first.

You made my whole being. You formed me in my mother's body. I praise you because you made me in an amazing and wonderful way. What you have done is wonderful.

— Psalm 139:13–14A (ICB)

When a sperm joins together with an egg, it is called *conception* or *fertilization*. The sperm and egg begin to grow together as one ball of cells. This ball of cells travels from the Fallopian tubes to the uterus. It's called an *embryo* and will stay in the uterus until the baby is ready to be born.

Of course, a baby is not made every time a husband and wife make love. It is just at special times when the sperm and egg are perfectly matched.

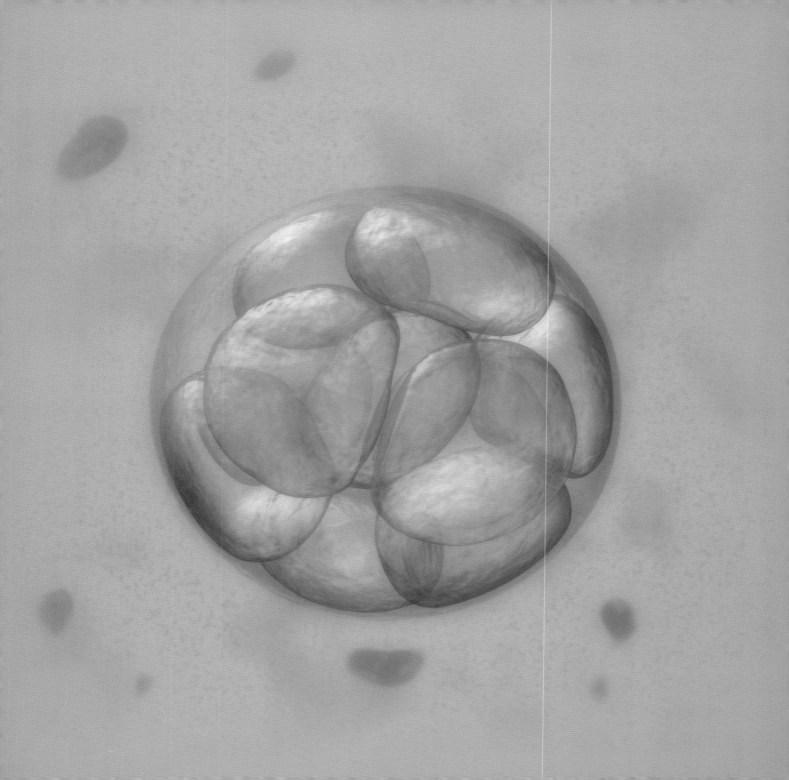

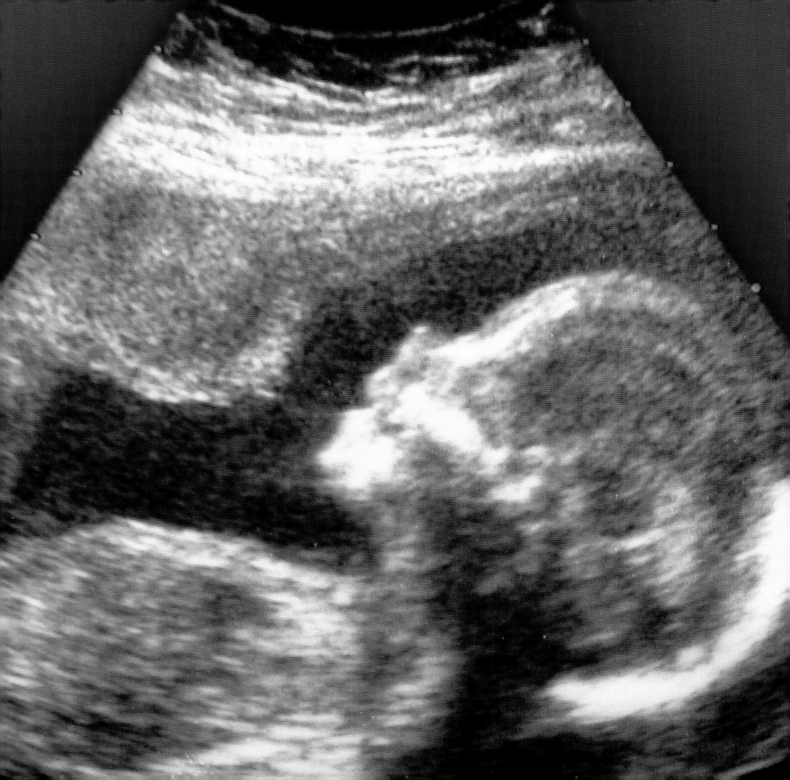

You saw my bones being formed as I took shape in my mother's body. When I was put together there, you saw my body as it was formed.

— Psalm 139:15–16A (ICB)

From the very moment the sperm and egg join together, so many details about the baby are already decided!

...if the baby is a boy or a girl

...what color her eyes will be

...what color hair (and how much!) he will have

...whether she will grow up to be tall or short

...if he will have big feet

...if she will have freckles

...and much more!

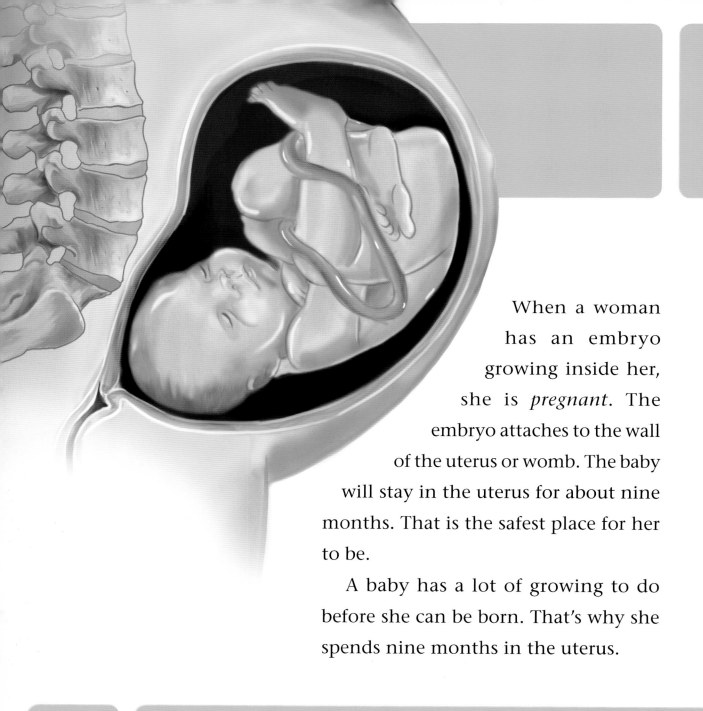

When a woman has an embryo growing inside her, she is *pregnant*. The embryo attaches to the wall of the uterus or womb. The baby will stay in the uterus for about nine months. That is the safest place for her to be.

A baby has a lot of growing to do before she can be born. That's why she spends nine months in the uterus.

As the baby grows, the mother's uterus grows too. It might look like her tummy is getting fat, but it's really the baby inside her getting bigger.

God planned for *everything* a baby needs in the uterus. All of the baby's nutrition comes from the mother through the *umbilical cord*. The umbilical cord is a twisty tube that connects the baby to the mother. Did you ever wonder why you have a belly button? That's where the umbilical cord was attached to your body!

A baby starts out so tiny that you almost can't see him. He is about the size of this dot: •

After one month, the baby has grown to about the size of a Cheerio. His backbone and arms and legs are beginning to form. He has a heart-beat, and blood is pumping through his tiny body.

Three Months

After three months in the uterus, the baby has a complete skeleton. She has feet and hands and toes and fingers. She can even suck her thumb! She's about the size of a large orange slice and is beginning to twist and turn inside her mother.

Six Months

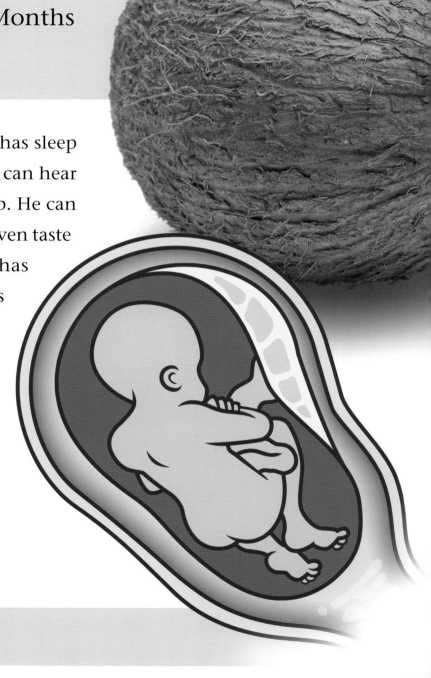

By six months, the baby has sleep time and awake time. He can hear sounds outside the womb. He can stick out his tongue and even taste something his mother has eaten. And he stretches and kicks so much that his mom can feel it! The baby has grown to be as long as a ruler. But he stays curled up in a ball about the size of a coconut.

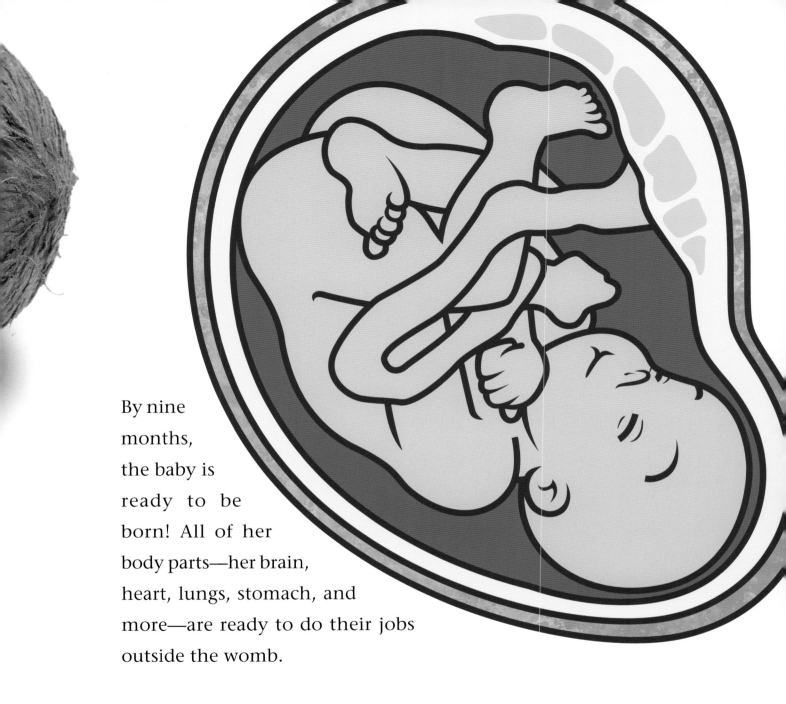

By nine months, the baby is ready to be born! All of her body parts—her brain, heart, lungs, stomach, and more—are ready to do their jobs outside the womb.

Nine Months

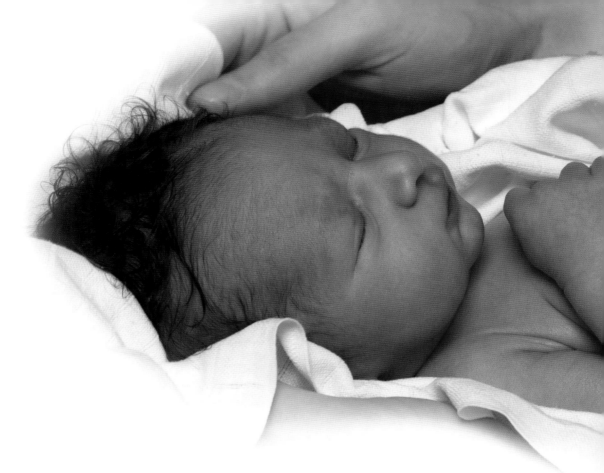

When a baby is ready to be born, the mother begins to feel *contractions*. This means the muscles in her uterus are getting ready to push the baby out. When a mother feels these contractions, she usually goes to a hospital.

It takes a lot of work for the mother to have a baby. In fact, it's called being *in labor* because the mother has to work so hard!

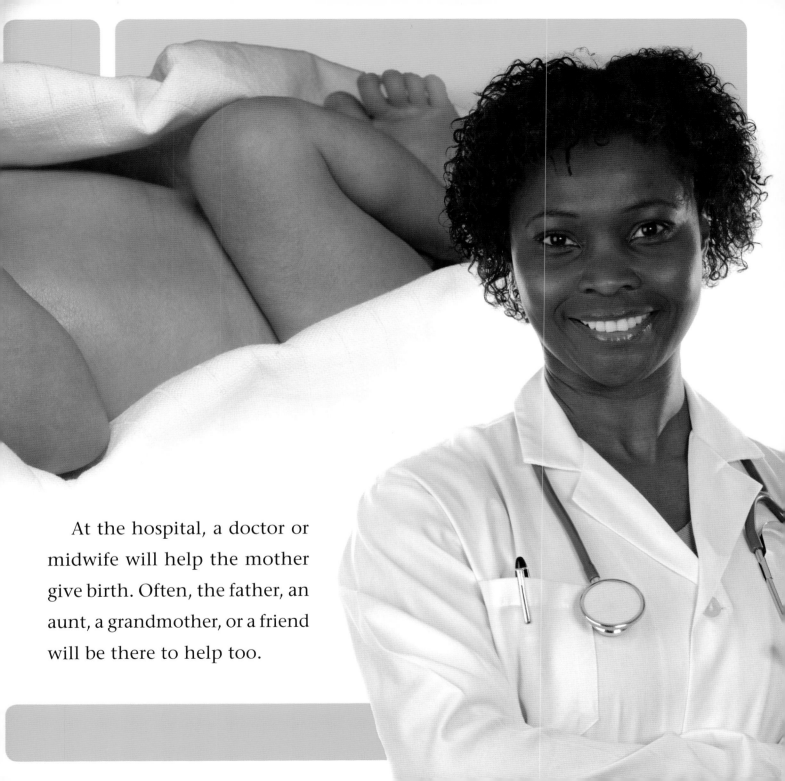

At the hospital, a doctor or midwife will help the mother give birth. Often, the father, an aunt, a grandmother, or a friend will be there to help too.

The contractions get stronger and stronger and finally push the baby out through the vagina.

Sometimes a baby can't come out through the mother's vagina. When this happens, a doctor will cut through the mother's skin and uterus. This is called a C-section. The baby is pulled out through this cut, and then the cut is sewed closed.

Now the baby is born! It's time to cut the umbilical cord—because now the baby can breathe through her nose and drink with her mouth.

After a few days in the hospital, it's time for the baby to go home with his family!

A brand-new baby needs a lot of care. He needs to be held and loved. He needs to be bathed and changed out of dirty diapers. He needs to be kept warm and safe. He needs to be fed.

A new baby gets all the nourishment he needs from milk that comes from the mother's breasts. Sometimes a baby will drink a special kind of milk, called *formula,* from a bottle. A baby's body isn't ready for foods like pizza or hamburgers or tacos until he is older.

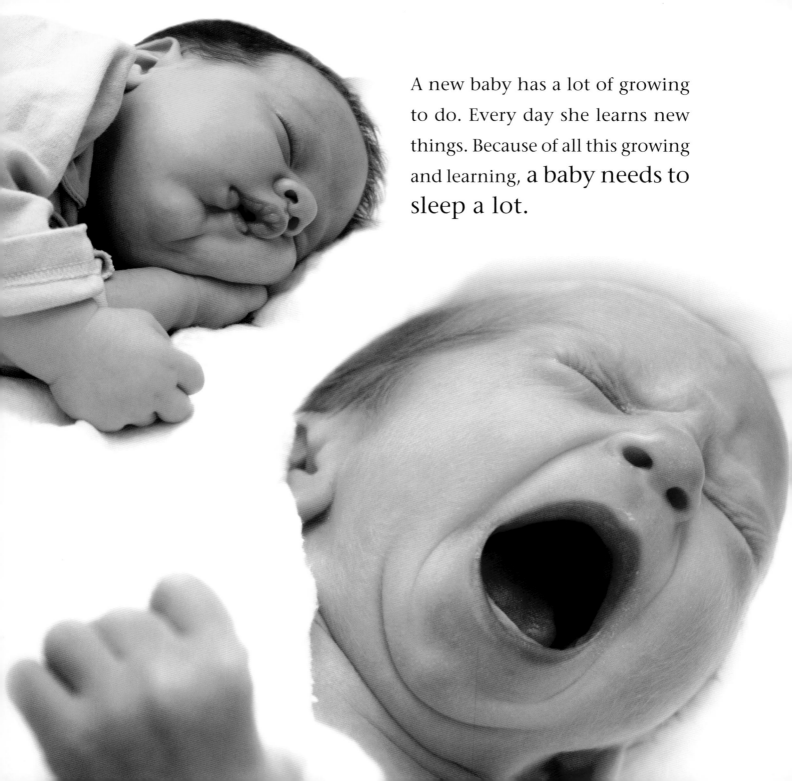

A new baby has a lot of growing to do. Every day she learns new things. Because of all this growing and learning, **a baby needs to sleep a lot.**

A new baby does a lot of crying too. She hasn't learned to talk yet, so crying is her way of telling her family she needs attention.

Having a new baby brings a lot of change to a family! But it will never change how much your family loves you.

God made families in all shapes and sizes, all colors and combinations. There are stepfamilies and extended families and families like no other. A family might have a mom and dad, or maybe just one or the other. Brothers and sisters, grandpas and grandmas, aunts and uncles and cousins—all of them can be part of a family.

W hat does your family look like? Are there lots of people in your family? Maybe it's just two or three of you.

No matter what your family looks like, you are God's gift to them. And they are God's gift to you.

God made your family! God made *you*.

God brought you into your family in a special way. Before you were born, God knew exactly who your family would be.

He had a perfect plan for you and your family!

Sometimes a baby or a child comes to a family in a special way called *adoption*.

Adoption is God's plan for when the birth mother and father—the ones who gave the egg and the sperm—cannot take care of the baby. The birth parents do a very loving and wonderful thing by allowing another family to adopt the baby. The new parents want to grow their family, and they welcome the baby into their home. The baby becomes their child. They love and take care of him just as they would love and take care of a child who was born to them.

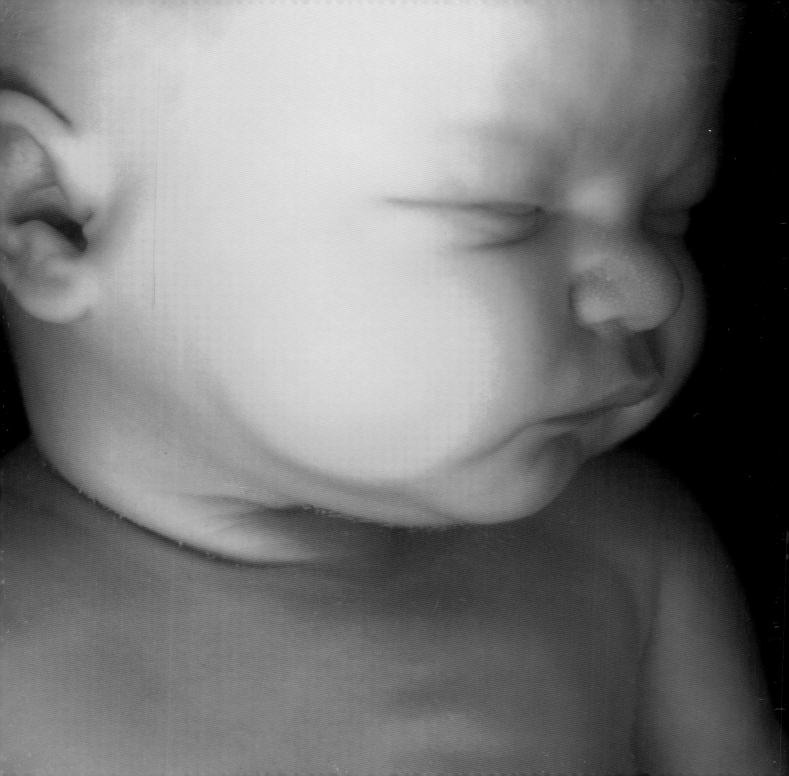

God makes babies in a miraculous way.
Every baby who ever was, was created by Him!
Thank you, God, for creating ME!

Before I formed you in the womb,
I knew you.
Before you were born,
I set you apart for my holy purpose.

JEREMIAH 1:5A (GW)

For Ages 3–5

For Ages 6–9

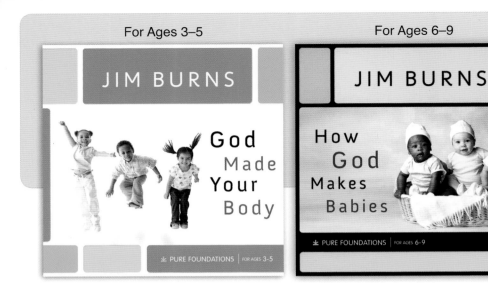

Dear Parents,

The dialogue doesn't stop here. By reading this book with your child, and by being open and honest when they ask questions, you're laying a foundation of trust that will extend into your child's preteen and teen years. To keep the conversation going, I invite you to check out the other books in the PURE FOUNDATIONS series.

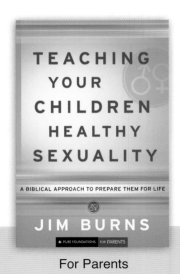

For Ages 10–14

For Ages 14+

For Parents